Together We Learn™

Reading For Understand

CW00686915

Table of Contents

Context Clues

Sequence

Cause and Effect

Drawing Conclusions

Realism/Fantasy

Fact and Opinion

Classify

Compare and Contrast

Predict

Main Idea and Supporting Details

© Disney

In Other Words

Help Tuck and Roll use **context clues** to figure out the meaning of some words on this sign. Using context clues means using words and sentences around the unknown word to help you figure out the meaning.

Fill in the circle beside the word that means the same thing as the word on the sign with the matching number.

> ## BUG CIRCUS
>
> Come one, come all to P.T. Flea's **marvelous**[1] circus! You will laugh when you see the **hilarious**[2] clown act. You will be **amazed**[3] at the magic of Manny. See the acrobats Tuck and Roll **perform**[4] an act you will never forget. Be **prepared**[5] to be **terrified**[6] by Rosie's wild insect taming act. Hurry! Come today!

1. ○ wonderful
   ○ bad

2. ○ old
   ○ funny

3. ○ bored
   ○ surprised

4. ○ do
   ○ see

5. ○ late
   ○ ready

6. ○ scared
   ○ lazy

Context Clues

© Disney/Pixar

Following the Rules Is Easy!

Tuck and Roll want to follow the rules. But they are having trouble with this sign in the lunchroom. You can help them.

Fill in the circle beside the word that means the same thing as the word on the sign with the matching number.

LUNCHROOM RULES

- Always leave the lunchroom **tidy**.
  1
- Rinse your leaves after you **complete** your meal.
  2
- We hope you will **enjoy** your lunch.
  3

1. ◯ neat
   ◯ messy

2. ◯ pay for
   ◯ finish

3. ◯ like
   ◯ forget

© Disney/Pixar

Context Clues

3

Nice Day for a Walk

Name

Read the story about Pongo and Perdita.

One day Pongo and Perdita took their pups for a walk. First, they walked through the park. Then they played in the field. Last, they strolled by the river. They had a nice day.

Number the events from the story in the order they happened. Write **1** by the first event, **2** by the second event, and **3** by the third event. The clue words **first**, **then**, and **last** will help you.

_____ They played in the field.

_____ They strolled by the river.

_____ They took a walk in the park.

Sequence

© Disney

Let's Put Things in Order

Read the story about Peter Pan and Wendy.

Peter Pan is looking for his shadow. First, he flies to the Darling house. Next, he finds his shadow. Finally, Wendy sews his shadow back on to him.

Number the events from the story in the order they happen. Write **1** by the first event, **2** by the second event, and **3** by the third event. The clue words **first**, **next**, and **finally** will help you.

_____ Wendy sews Peter's shadow back onto him.

_____ Peter flies to the Darling house.

_____ Peter finds his shadow.

© Disney

Sequence

5

First Things First

Cinderella does so many jobs! Some jobs have many steps. Help Cinderella know the order she should follow to get each job done. Write the words **first**, **next**, and **last** to show the order of each job. Remember to begin each sentence with a capital letter.

Making Breakfast

_____, cook the oatmeal.

_____, pour oatmeal and water into a pan.

_____, bring the oatmeal to the table.

Washing the Floor

_____, rinse the floor with clean water.

_____, wash the floor with soapy water.

_____, sweep the floor.

Sequence

© Disney

A Day in the Jungle

Name _____

Living in the jungle can be exciting! Use the clue words **first**, **then**, and **finally** to give you clues about the order of things that happened in Tarzan's jungle. Read the story below. Then answer the questions.

Jane had an exciting day. First, she drew a picture of a baby baboon. Then angry baboons began to chase Jane. Finally, Tarzan picked up Jane and carried her away from the baboons.

What happened last? _____

_____

What happened second? _____

_____

What happened first? _____

_____

Run for Cover!

A **cause** is why something happened. An **effect** is what happened. Read the story about Pumbaa.

Nala jumped out at Pumbaa. Pumbaa was afraid that Nala would eat him, so he ran away. He crawled under a fallen tree, but he was too big. He got stuck.

Each of these sentences begins with an effect. Underline a cause to complete each sentence.

1. Pumbaa ran away
   a. because he wanted to play a game with Nala.

   b. because he was afraid of Nala.

2. Pumbaa got stuck
   a. because he was too big to fit under the fallen tree.

   b. because he could not run fast enough.

Cause and Effect

© Disney

Try Harder, Simba

Name

Read the story about Mufasa and Simba.

Mufasa told Simba to go home and stay away from danger. Simba disobeyed his father and got into trouble. Mufasa rescued Simba. Then he scolded Simba for disobeying him. Simba decided to try harder to be good.

Each of these sentences begins with a cause. Underline an effect to complete each sentence.

1. Because Simba disobeyed Mufasa,
    a. Mufasa scolded Simba.

    b. Mufasa was proud of Simba.

2. Because Simba wanted to please Mufasa,
    a. Simba disobeyed him.

    b. Simba decided to try harder to be good.

© Disney

Cause and Effect

Watch Mulan Climb

Read the story about Mulan. Think about causes and effects.

Mulan wants to climb the tall pole. She practices climbing every day. At last, she can reach the top!

Complete the sentences by writing a cause or an effect.

1. Mulan practices climbing every day because

_____

_____

2. Because Mulan practices climbing every day

_____

_____

Cause and Effect

© Disney

A Puzzle for Snow White

Name _____

Snow White received four gifts from four dwarfs. She knows that each gift came from a different dwarf. Use these clues to help her figure out who gave each gift.

Clues

1. Doc likes to read.
2. Sleepy likes to take long naps.
3. Sneezy seems to have a cold that never ends.
4. Bashful likes pretty flowers.

Draw a line from the picture of the dwarf to the gift he gave Snow White.

Doc

Sleepy

Sneezy

Bashful

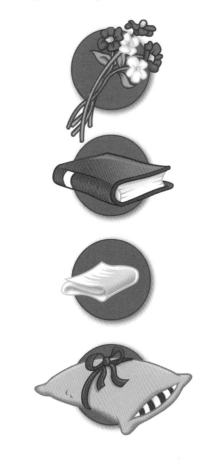

© Disney

Drawing Conclusions

11

Solving Mysteries

Raising so many puppies keeps Pongo and Perdita on their toes. Every day they solve little mysteries. To help them solve the mystery of the missing sandwich, read this list of clues.

Clue 1:
The sandwich was on the table only a few minutes ago.

Clue 2:
All the puppies except Lucky and Penny went outside to play about one hour ago.

Clue 3:
Lucky has jelly on his face.

Who took the sandwich? Use the clues to help you decide. Circle the conclusion that makes the most sense.

a. Penny took the sandwich and buried it.

b. Lucky took the sandwich and ate it.

c. One of the other puppies took the sandwich outside.

Drawing Conclusions

© Disney

Tarzan and Clayton

Name

Read this story about Tarzan and Clayton. Then circle the correct answer following each question.

Tarzan trusted Clayton, but Clayton fooled Tarzan. He locked Tarzan in a ship. Then Clayton captured Tarzan's friends.

1. Did Clayton lie to Tarzan?

   a. Yes, Clayton lied.   b. No, Clayton didn't lie.

2. Is Clayton an honest person?

   a. Yes, Clayton is honest.   b. No, Clayton is not honest.

3. Would Tarzan trust Clayton the next time?

   a. Yes, Tarzan would   b. No, Tarzan would
      trust Clayton.   not trust Clayton.

© Burroughs and Disney
TARZAN®

Drawing Conclusions

Could It Happen?

Some events in a story could really happen. They are **realistic**. Other story events could never happen in real life. They are **fantastic**.

Examples:
Realistic — Rain fell from the sky.
Fantastic — Each raindrop changed into a diamond.

Read this list of events. Underline the realistic events—those that could really happen.

1. Pocahontas paddled her canoe on the river.

2. The canoe turned into a giant eagle.

3. Pocahontas paddled her canoe to the moon.

4. The raccoon climbed a tree.

5. The birds built a nest on a tree branch.

Draw a picture of one realistic event from the list.

14   Realism/Fantasy

© Disney

This Is Fantastic! _____

Here are other examples of realistic and fantastic events.

Examples:
Realistic — The boy took a walk.
Fantastic — The trees took a walk.

Read this list of events. Underline the fantastic events—those that could never happen in real life.

1. The snake slid through the tall grass.

2. The panther used his wings to help him fly high above the jungle.

3. Mowgli sang a happy song.

4. The elephants rode a bus to get through the jungle.

5. The bananas begged Baloo not to eat them.

Draw a picture of one event from the list that could never happen in real life.

© Disney

Realism/Fantasy

15

Is That a Fact?

Name

A statement of **fact** can be proven true or false. An **opinion** tells what one person thinks, feels, or believes. It cannot be proven.

Read this conversation between Belle and the Beast. Underline each statement of fact. Circle each sentence that is an opinion.

1. "I think that today was wonderful."

2. "The sun shone all day."

3. "I liked the picnic."

4. "I loved the food."

5. "We went home in the afternoon."

Fact and Opinion

© Disney

Nice job!

Excellent!

Amazing!

Magnificent!

You're on top!

Way to go!

Wonderful!

Beautiful work!

Great job!

Purrr-fect!

31326-630

Well done!

Good for you!

Fantastic!

Good thinking!

Splendid!

Tigger-ific!

Lookin' good!

Just lovely!

Marvelous!

A honey of a job!

What Is Your Opinion?

Read this letter that Belle wrote to her father. It is filled with statements of facts and opinions. Underline each statement of fact. Circle each sentence that is an opinion.

Dear Father,

You would like this castle. It has towers that are about 50 feet high. My room has two windows that face east. The garden has many kinds of flowers. I think they are so beautiful.

Sometimes the castle feels lonely to me. But I think the Beast is nicer than he seemed at first.

Your loving daughter,

Belle

© Disney

Fact and Opinion

Under the Sea or on the Land?

Name _____

Help Ariel color the things that belong under the sea. Draw an **X** on the things that belong on land.

Classify

© Disney

Name _____

© Disney

Classify

Plant or Animal?

Name

Many plants and animals live in the forest. Draw an **X** on each animal. Circle each plant.

20

Classify

© Disney

In the Circus or on the Farm?

Help Dumbo sort words that name things that belong in the circus. Write the words that belong in the circus on the lines.

Mrs. Jumbo	barn	tractor	scarecrow
the Ringmaster	garden	tent	clown

In the Circus

_____

_____

_____

_____

Where do you think the other words belong? Unscramble these letters to find out.

F R M A

___ ___ ___ ___

Classify

© Disney

21

Alike or Different?

Name _____

When you tell how two things are alike, you **compare** them. When you tell how two things are different, you **contrast** them. Complete the sentences. Write color words to compare and contrast.

1. Woody's hat and boots are alike because they are both _____.

2. Woody's shirt and pants are different because his shirt is _____ and his pants are _____.

3. Rex and the Green Army men are alike because they are both _____.

4. Bullseye is different from Hamm because Bullseye is _____ and Hamm is _____.

Compare and Contrast

Toy Story 2 © Disney/Pixar
Original _Toy Story_ Elements © Disney
All rights reserved.

Toy Pals

_____

Name

Read this paragraph.
Then answer the questions below.

Woody and Buzz Lightyear are both toys. They both belong to Andy. Woody is a cowboy. Buzz is a space ranger. Woody wears jeans and a cowboy hat. Buzz wears a space suit with a helmet.

1. What are two ways that Woody and Buzz Lightyear are alike?

_____

_____

_____

_____

2. What are two ways that Woody and Buzz Lightyear are different?

_____

_____

_____

_____

© Disney

Compare and Contrast

Friendly Fairies

Read this paragraph about Flora and Merryweather. Then answer the questions below.

Flora and Merryweather are both good fairies. Flora has gray hair. She wears pink clothes. Merryweather has black hair. She wears blue clothes. They may look different, but they both love Aurora very much.

1. What are two ways that Flora and Merryweather are alike?

_____

_____

_____

_____

2. What are two ways that Flora and Merryweather are different?

_____

_____

_____

_____

24   Compare and Contrast   © Disney

Guess What Happens Next

To **predict** means to tell what you think might happen next. Read each story. Then predict what will happen. Fill in the circle next to the correct answer.

Cruella De Vil is a very evil person. She wants a new fur coat to wear. She sees the Dalmatian puppies with their pretty fur coats. What will she do?

1. ○ She will be kind to the puppies.

2. ○ She will try to steal the puppies for their fur.

Pongo and Perdita love their puppies very much. They worried about them when they were gone. Now, they have their puppies back home. What will Pongo and Perdita do?

1. ○ They will feel very happy and will stay close to their puppies.

2. ○ They will leave their puppies alone every day.

© Disney

Predict

25

Be Good, Pinocchio

Name

Read each story. Then predict what will happen next. Fill in the circle next to the correct answer.

Jiminy Cricket always helps Pinocchio choose the right thing to do. J. Worthington Foulfellow has asked Pinocchio to skip school with him. What will Jiminy do?

1. ○ He will tell Pinocchio to go to school.

2. ○ He will tell Pinocchio to take the day off and have some fun.

The Blue Fairy is very proud of Pinocchio. He has been brave and has tried hard to be good. She knows that he always wanted to be a real boy. What will the Blue Fairy do?

1. ○ She will scold him.

2. ○ She will wave her wand and make him a real boy.

26

Predict

© Disney

What I'm Trying to Say Is . . .

The **main idea** of a paragraph is its most important idea. **Supporting details** are bits of information that tell more about the main idea. The underlined sentence is the main idea in the following example.

Example: Pizza Planet is exciting. It is colorful and noisy. It has lots of games to play.

Read this paragraph. Look for the main idea. Fill in the circle next to the paragraph's main idea.

Woody is a good leader. All the other toys listen to him because he is kind and smart. He comes up with good ways to solve everyone's problems.

1. ○ Woody comes up with good ways to solve everyone's problems.

2. ○ Woody is a good leader.

3. ○ All the other toys listen to Woody because he is kind and smart.

© Disney

Main Idea and Supporting Details

27

Tell Me More

Aladdin is telling Jasmine about a place he has been. Read the paragraph. Look for the main idea and the supporting details. Then follow the directions under the story.

It was a terrible place. The snow was deep and cold. The strong wind almost froze me. The sky was full of dark clouds.

1. Circle the sentence that tells the main idea.

2. Underline the supporting details that tell about the main idea.

3. Write your own sentence to add a supporting detail to Aladdin's story.

_____

_____

_____

Main Idea and Supporting Details

© Disney

The Amazing and Powerful Genie

Name

Read this paragraph. Look for the main idea and the supporting details. Then follow the directions under the paragraph.

The Genie can do many things. He can make himself bigger or smaller. He can make himself look like other people or things. He can make copies of himself.

1. Write the sentence that tells the main idea of the paragraph.

   _____

2. Underline the supporting details that tell more about the main idea.

3. Write one of the detail sentences. Draw a picture to go with it.

   _____

   _____

Helping Your Child at Home

Reading for Understanding

Helping your child develop reading comprehension skills is critical to his or her success in school. You can help your child develop these important skills through the lessons in this book and the suggestions below:

- **Context Clues:** When you hear a new word on the TV or the radio, ask your child to guess what it may mean, based on the context in which you heard it.

- **Sequence:** Cut up a three- or four-panel newspaper cartoon. Ask your child to arrange the pictures in an order that makes sense. Have him or her retell the story using the clue words *first*, *next*, *then*, and *last* or *finally*.

- **Cause and Effect:** While watching a video, pause it occasionally and ask, "What happened?" and "Why did that happen?"

- **Drawing Conclusions:** When your child misplaces something, prompt him or her with clues such as "Where did you see it last?" or "Who else might have used it?" Help him or her draw a conclusion about where the missing item may be now.

- **Realism and fantasy:** Give your child two signs—one labeled *R* for realistic and the other labeled *F* for fantastic. Next, suggest various realistic or fantastic events such as "You will ride the bus to school tomorrow" or "We will climb a giant beanstalk to the clouds tonight." Have him or her hold up the appropriate sign to describe the event. Then, switch roles.

- **Fact and Opinion:** Occasionally, pause conversation at dinner and ask your child if what was just said was a fact or an opinion.

- **Classify:** Ask your child to help with classifying jobs such as putting away the silverware in the appropriate parts of the silverware drawer or folding the clean clothes according to type of clothing.

- **Compare and Contrast:** On walks with your child, ask him or her to point out how specific houses, cars, trees, or gardens are alike and how they are different.

- **Predict:** Pause a video that you both are watching and ask your child to predict what might happen next. Then, verify the prediction.

- **Main Idea and Supporting Details:** Supply your child with simple main ideas, and ask him or her to add supporting details. For example, you might say, "This movie was funny. Tell me what was funny about it."

© Disney

Page 2

1. wonderful
2. funny
3. surprised
4. do
5. ready
6. scared

Page 3

1. neat
2. finish
3. like

Page 4

2
3
1

Page 5

3
1
2

Page 6

Making Breakfast

Next

First

Last

Washing the Floor

Last

Next

First

Page 7

last, Tarzan picked up Jane and carried her away from the baboons.

second, Angry baboons began to chase Jane.

first, Jane drew a picture of a baby baboon.

Page 8

1. b.
2. a.

Page 9

1. a.
2. b.

Page 10

1. she wants to climb the tall pole.

2. she can reach the top.

Page 11

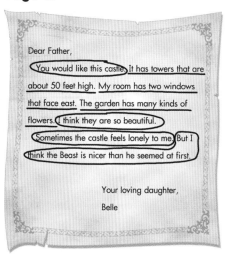

Doc
Sleepy
Sneezy
Bashful

Page 12

b. Lucky took the sandwich and ate it.

Page 13

1. a.
2. b.
3. b.

Page 14

1.
4.
5.

Page 15

2.
4.
5.

Page 16

Underline 2 and 5.

Circle 1, 3, and 4.

Page 17

Dear Father,

You would like this castle. It has towers that are about 50 feet high. My room has two windows that face east. The garden has many kinds of flowers. I think they are so beautiful. Sometimes the castle feels lonely to me. But I think the Beast is nicer than he seemed at first.

Your loving daughter,

Belle

© Disney

Pages 18 and 19

Color King Triton, Flounder, the sea horses, the dolphin, and Ursula.

Put an **X** on Max, the horse, Eric, and the flowers.

Page 20

Draw an **X** on Bambi, Flower, Thumper, the butterfly, and the bird.

Circle the trees, the flowers, and the grass.

Page 21

In the Circus

Mrs. Jumbo

the ringmaster

tent

clown

Unscrambled letters

FARM

Page 22

1. brown

2. gold and orange; blue

3. green

4. brown; pink

Page 23

1. They are both toys.
   They both belong to Andy.

2. Possible answers:
   Woody is a cowboy;
   Buzz is a Space ranger.

   Woody wears a cowboy hat;
   Buzz wears a helmet.

Page 24

1. They are both good fairies.
   They both love Aurora.

2. Flora has gray hair;
   Merryweather has black hair.

   Flora wears pink;
   Merryweather wears blue.

Page 25

Cruella: 2.

Pongo and Perdita: 1.

Page 26

Jiminy Cricket: 1.

The Blue Fairy: 2.

Page 27

2. Woody is a good leader.

Page 28

It was a terrible place. The snow was deep and cold. The strong wind almost froze me. The sky was full of dark clouds.

3. Possible answer:
   There was no one around to help me.

Page 29

1. The Genie can do many things.

2. The Genie can do many things. He can make himself bigger or smaller. He can make himself look like other people or things. He can make copies of himself.

3. Answers may vary. Possible answers include any of the underlined details in number 2.

© Disney